CPSIA information can be obtained
at www.ICGtesting.com
Printed in the USA
BVHW042148050619
550326BV00013B/145/P

9 781095 886786